Subtraction Booster

Subtraction Booster provides students with focused practice to help reinforce and develop subtraction skills. Exercises are grade-level appropriate, with clear examples and instructions, and are designed in accordance with national standards. They include a variety of activities to help students develop their subtraction and other basic math skills.

Subtraction Booster is fact filled and fast paced to keep learning interesting, fun, and exciting while students improve their ability to do math.

All rights reserved
Copyright 2005 Cookie Jar Publishing

Cookie Jar Publishing™ grants the right to the purchaser to reproduce materials in this book for noncommercial individual or classroom use. Reproduction for an entire school or school system is prohibited. No part of this publication may be otherwise reproduced for storage in a retrieval system or transmitted in any form or by any means, electronic, mechanical, recording, or otherwise, without prior written permission of the publisher.

For information, write:
Cookie Jar Publishing • 332 West Martin Lane • Salt Lake City, UT 84107

ISBN: 1-59441-342-8

PRINTED IN THE UNITED STATES OF AMERICA
10 9 8 7 6 5 4 3 2 1

Table of Contents

Problem Solving............ 3–6

Writing Numbers:
   0 to 49 7
   50 to 99 8

Problem Solving............. 9

Word Problem Solving....... 10

Writing Numbers:
   100 to 149 11
   150 to 199 12

Problem Solving......... 13–14

Matching Equations and
   Answers............ 15–16

Problem Solving......... 17–18

Writing Numbers:
   200 to 249 19
   250 to 299 20

Word Problem Solving....... 21

Changing Number Words
   to Numerals............ 22

Writing Numbers:
   300 to 349 23
   350 to 399 24

Subtracting
   2-Digit Numbers 25–27

Writing Numbers:
   400 to 449 28
   450 to 499 29

Subtracting
   3-Digit Numbers 30–31

Brain Teasers 32–39
   Dot-to-Dot.............. 32
   Money Math 33
   Telling Time............ 34
   Picture Problems 35
   Greater Than or Less Than. 36
   Popcorn Problems 37
   Crossword Puzzle..... 38–39

Subtracting
   3-Digit Numbers 40

Writing Numbers:
   500 to 549 41
   550 to 599 42
   600 to 649 43
   650 to 699 44

Fractions
   Identifying Fractions 45
   Writing Fractions 46

2-Digit Subtraction
   with Regrouping 47–49
   with Some Regrouping 50–51

Problem Solving............ 52

Word Problem Solving.... 53–54

Problem Solving............ 55

3-Digit Subtraction
   with Regrouping 56–57
   with Some Regrouping ... 58

Answer Pages........... 59–63

Problem Solving

Write the difference.

1.
   10 − 1 = **9**
   4 − 4 = 0
   6 − 0 = 6
   9 − 6 = 3
   8 − 2 = 6

2.
   5 − 4 = 1
   11 − 0 = 11
   2 − 1 = 1
   5 − 2 = 3
   10 − 4 = 6

3.
   12 − 2 = 10
   10 − 8 = 2
   7 − 2 = 5
   6 − 3 = 3
   11 − 5 = 6

4.
   6 − 2 = 4
   11 − 2 = 9
   1 − 0 = 1
   5 − 4 = 1
   12 − 7 = 5

5.
   12 − 0 = 12
   7 − 3 = 4
   0 − 0 =
   2 − 2 =
   10 − 7 =

Problem Solving

Write the difference.

1. $\begin{array}{r} 9 \\ -1 \\ \hline 8 \end{array}$ $\begin{array}{r} 10 \\ -5 \\ \hline \end{array}$ $\begin{array}{r} 7 \\ -4 \\ \hline \end{array}$ $\begin{array}{r} 6 \\ -6 \\ \hline \end{array}$ $\begin{array}{r} 8 \\ -0 \\ \hline \end{array}$

2. $\begin{array}{r} 7 \\ -7 \\ \hline \end{array}$ $\begin{array}{r} 4 \\ -3 \\ \hline \end{array}$ $\begin{array}{r} 10 \\ -3 \\ \hline \end{array}$ $\begin{array}{r} 6 \\ -4 \\ \hline \end{array}$ $\begin{array}{r} 3 \\ -3 \\ \hline \end{array}$

3. $\begin{array}{r} 9 \\ -3 \\ \hline \end{array}$ $\begin{array}{r} 10 \\ -6 \\ \hline \end{array}$ $\begin{array}{r} 12 \\ -4 \\ \hline \end{array}$ $\begin{array}{r} 5 \\ -3 \\ \hline \end{array}$ $\begin{array}{r} 6 \\ -5 \\ \hline \end{array}$

4. $\begin{array}{r} 8 \\ -2 \\ \hline \end{array}$ $\begin{array}{r} 11 \\ -7 \\ \hline \end{array}$ $\begin{array}{r} 9 \\ -4 \\ \hline \end{array}$ $\begin{array}{r} 6 \\ -3 \\ \hline \end{array}$ $\begin{array}{r} 8 \\ -5 \\ \hline \end{array}$

5. $\begin{array}{r} 7 \\ -5 \\ \hline \end{array}$ $\begin{array}{r} 8 \\ -1 \\ \hline \end{array}$ $\begin{array}{r} 9 \\ -5 \\ \hline \end{array}$ $\begin{array}{r} 12 \\ -3 \\ \hline \end{array}$ $\begin{array}{r} 11 \\ -9 \\ \hline \end{array}$

Problem Solving

Write the difference.

1.
10 − 0 = __10__
5 − 1 = _____
11 − 3 = _____
10 − 2 = _____
2 − 0 = _____
4 − 1 = _____

2.
7 − 1 = _____
12 − 9 = _____
8 − 5 = _____
9 − 9 = _____
3 − 2 = _____
5 − 0 = _____

3.
8 − 6 = _____
12 − 11 = _____
1 − 1 = _____
9 − 5 = _____
10 − 3 = _____
9 − 2 = _____

4.
6 − 0 = _____
11 − 8 = _____
8 − 8 = _____
12 − 2 = _____
10 − 10 = _____
7 − 5 = _____

Problem Solving

Write the difference.

1.

11 − 1 = __10__
9 − 7 = _____
8 − 3 = _____
10 − 3 = _____
12 − 12 = _____
9 − 0 = _____

2.

3 − 0 = _____
11 − 4 = _____
9 − 8 = _____
12 − 1 = _____
11 − 6 = _____
9 − 2 = _____

3.

11 − 11 = _____
10 − 9 = _____
12 − 3 = _____
4 − 0 = _____
7 − 3 = _____
8 − 1 = _____

4.

4 − 2 = _____
12 − 5 = _____
8 − 4 = _____
5 − 5 = _____
9 − 2 = _____
11 − 10 = _____

Subtraction Booster—Grade 2
1-59441-342-8

Writing Numbers: 0 to 49

Start with 0. Write to 49.

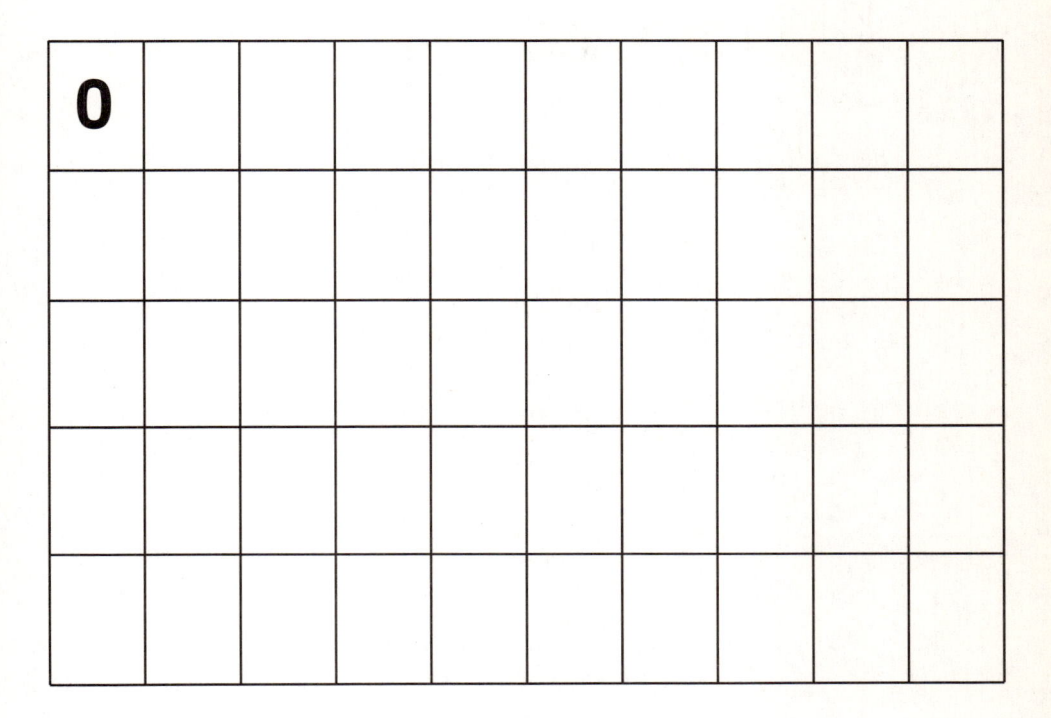

0									

1. What number comes before 47? _____

2. What number comes before 11? _____

3. What number comes between 27 and 29? _____

4. What number comes after 32? _____

Writing Numbers: 50 to 99

Start with 50. Write to 99.

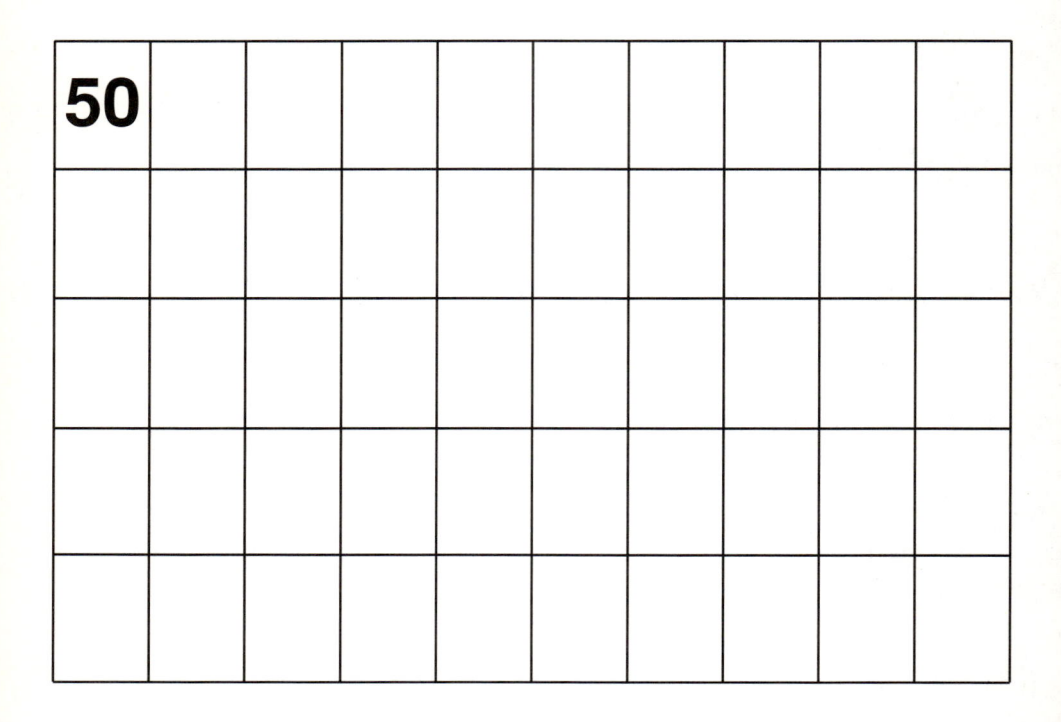

50									

1. What are the even numbers between 50 and 60?

50 _____ _____ _____ _____ 60.

2. What are the odd numbers between 81 and 91?

81 _____ _____ _____ _____ 91.

3. What is the next even number after 64? _____

Problem Solving

Solve each problem below.

1.
$$7 - 4 = 3$$ $$7 - 0$$ $$10 - 8$$ $$4 - 4$$ $$3 - 2$$

2.
$$11 - 8$$ $$8 - 1$$ $$9 - 2$$ $$6 - 2$$ $$4 - 1$$

3.
$$9 - 7$$ $$0 - 0$$ $$4 - 1$$ $$8 - 2$$ $$9 - 1$$

4.
$$6 - 2$$ $$1 - 1$$ $$7 - 3$$ $$6 - 0$$ $$12 - 1$$

5.
$$12 - 9$$ $$5 - 1$$ $$10 - 6$$ $$7 - 3$$ $$10 - 2$$

Word Problem Solving

Read the story. Write the problem and the answer.

1. LeeAnn fed the neighbors' dogs while they were on a trip. She fed 9 dogs in the morning and only 7 dogs at night. How many dogs did not eat at night?

   $9 - 7 = 2$

2. Dianne planted 5 roses in her flower garden. 3 roses were red. The rest of them were pink. How many roses were pink?

3. 10 nuts were on the ground. The chipmunks ate 7 of them. How many nuts were left on the ground?

4. Trent got a new box of 12 crayons. 6 of them were broken. How many crayons were not broken?

Writing Numbers: 100 to 149

Start with 100. Write to 149.

100				

Writing Numbers: 150 to 199

Start with 150. Write to 199.

150					

Problem Solving

Solve each problem by writing the difference.

1.
   15   13   16   18   17
 − 8   − 7   − 4   − 18   − 6
   7

2.
   14   16   15   13   18
 − 11   − 2   − 15   − 9   − 5

3.
   17   16   14   17   16
 − 0   − 10   − 3   − 10   − 0

4.
   14   15   15   12   18
 − 7   − 6   − 11   − 10   − 2

Problem Solving

Solve each problem by writing the difference.

1. $\begin{array}{r}16\\-7\\\hline 9\end{array}$ $\begin{array}{r}13\\-2\\\hline\end{array}$ $\begin{array}{r}18\\-16\\\hline\end{array}$ $\begin{array}{r}14\\-5\\\hline\end{array}$ $\begin{array}{r}15\\-12\\\hline\end{array}$

2. $\begin{array}{r}18\\-1\\\hline\end{array}$ $\begin{array}{r}14\\-9\\\hline\end{array}$ $\begin{array}{r}16\\-3\\\hline\end{array}$ $\begin{array}{r}17\\-8\\\hline\end{array}$ $\begin{array}{r}14\\-10\\\hline\end{array}$

3. $\begin{array}{r}15\\-13\\\hline\end{array}$ $\begin{array}{r}13\\-6\\\hline\end{array}$ $\begin{array}{r}18\\-7\\\hline\end{array}$ $\begin{array}{r}15\\-9\\\hline\end{array}$ $\begin{array}{r}18\\-12\\\hline\end{array}$

4. $\begin{array}{r}13\\-10\\\hline\end{array}$ $\begin{array}{r}17\\-13\\\hline\end{array}$ $\begin{array}{r}15\\-4\\\hline\end{array}$ $\begin{array}{r}14\\-12\\\hline\end{array}$ $\begin{array}{r}18\\-4\\\hline\end{array}$

5. $\begin{array}{r}17\\-11\\\hline\end{array}$ $\begin{array}{r}15\\-15\\\hline\end{array}$ $\begin{array}{r}14\\-6\\\hline\end{array}$ $\begin{array}{r}17\\-2\\\hline\end{array}$ $\begin{array}{r}12\\-4\\\hline\end{array}$

Matching Equations and Answers

Draw a line to the answer for each problem.

1.

16 − 12 =	7
14 − 7 =	5
18 − 17 =	4
15 − 10 =	1
13 − 11 =	2

2.

18 − 3 =	15
15 − 7 =	1
14 − 4 =	8
13 − 12 =	10
16 − 8 =	8

3.

17 − 4 =	11
13 − 3 =	18
16 − 5 =	10
15 − 14 =	13
18 − 0 =	1

4.

14 − 13 =	8
13 − 4 =	1
16 − 9 =	9
15 − 3 =	7
17 − 9 =	12

5.

16 − 1 =	1
13 − 8 =	5
16 − 15 =	12
18 − 6 =	15
17 − 7 =	10

6.

16 − 11 =	1
14 − 13 =	5
18 − 8 =	9
17 − 8 =	10
14 − 1 =	13

Matching Equations and Answers

Draw a line to the answer for each problem.

1.

18 − 2 =	13
13 − 5 =	8
15 − 2 =	9
16 − 6 =	10
18 − 9 =	16

2.

14 − 13 =	2
16 − 14 =	10
18 − 8 =	4
18 − 14 =	0
13 − 13 =	1

3.

16 − 16 =	12
15 − 1 =	13
17 − 5 =	14
18 − 11 =	0
13 − 0 =	7

4.

18 − 10 =	8
13 − 1 =	4
17 − 17 =	12
15 − 11 =	13
16 − 3 =	0

5.

17 − 12 =	3
13 − 5 =	5
18 − 15 =	9
16 − 7 =	8
18 − 4 =	14

6.

18 − 13 =	12
13 − 6 =	8
16 − 4 =	4
14 − 6 =	7
15 − 11 =	5

Problem Solving

Solve each problem below.

1.   17   18   11   7   16
       −11   −0   −4   −6   −11
        6

2.   18   11   8   16   14
       −4   −3   −8   −9   −5

3.   14   15   9   18   9
       −4   −12   −7   −12   −6

4.   17   9   15   16   16
       −10   −9   −0   −7   −0

5.   18   15   14   16   12
       −6   −10   −4   −6   −3

6.   14   13   15   16   11
       −9   −5   −9   −8   −2

Problem Solving

Solve each problem below.

1.
$$15 - 2 = 13$$ $$16 - 5$$ $$14 - 11$$ $$13 - 7$$ $$10 - 7$$

2.
$$12 - 4$$ $$18 - 17$$ $$13 - 6$$ $$12 - 7$$ $$13 - 2$$

3.
$$18 - 11$$ $$13 - 10$$ $$14 - 3$$ $$18 - 0$$ $$17 - 3$$

4.
$$18 - 1$$ $$14 - 14$$ $$12 - 4$$ $$13 - 1$$ $$14 - 7$$

5.
$$14 - 2$$ $$15 - 4$$ $$15 - 7$$ $$13 - 4$$ $$12 - 5$$

Writing Numbers: 200 to 249

Start with 200. Write to 249.

200					

Writing Numbers: 250 to 299

Start with 250. Write to 299.

250					

Word Problem Solving

Read the story. Write the problem and the answer on the line or in the box.

1. The children in room 9 go to school at 9:00. They go to lunch at 12:00. How many hours have they been in school before they go to lunch?

   12 − 9 = 3

2. The children get out of school at 3:00. Joe had to leave at 1:00. How much school did he miss?

3. 19 children each had to do a report. 8 children did reports on butterflies. How many children did not do reports on butterflies?

4. After recess the children read to themselves. Scott read 12 pages, and his friend read 9 pages. How many more pages did Scott read?

Changing Number Words to Numerals

Write the number after the number word.

1.

one	1
ten	_____
six	_____
four	_____
nine	_____

2.

five	_____
zero	_____
eleven	_____
seven	_____
two	_____
eight	_____

3.

three	_____
fourteen	_____
thirty	_____
sixteen	_____
fifty	_____

4.

thirty-one	_____
thirteen	_____
forty-three	_____
eighty-nine	_____
twenty-four	_____

5.

seventy-five	_____
twenty-nine	_____
sixty-seven	_____
eighteen	_____
sixty-eight	_____

6.

ninety-nine	_____
fifteen	_____
eighty-eight	_____
one hundred	_____
seventeen	_____

Subtraction Booster—Grade 2

1-59441-342-8

Writing Numbers: 300 to 349

Start with 300. Write to 349.

300					

Writing Numbers: 350 to 399

Start with 350. Write to 399.

350					

Subtracting 2-Digit Numbers

Write the difference. Subtract the ones column first.

ones column ↓

1.   24   64   83   46   87
    − 14   − 24   − 32   − 15   − 32
      10

2.   98   32   57   75   29
    − 84   − 12   − 34   − 62   − 19

3.   59   18   80   37   66
    − 53   − 2   − 30   − 14   − 22

4.   16   88   99   48   62
    − 6   − 44   − 35   − 26   − 12

5.   38   72   96   44   65
    − 16   − 32   − 13   − 12   − 10

Subtracting 2-Digit Numbers

Write the difference. Subtract the ones column first.

ones column ↓

1.
    27 72 33 45 39
  − 24 −21 −20 − 5 −17
    3

2.
    39 50 77 81 28
  − 38 − 40 − 25 − 30 − 12

3.
    94 63 36 10 47
  − 82 − 43 − 34 − 5 − 16

4.
    81 25 55 82 69
  − 41 − 24 − 40 − 10 − 24

5.
    75 19 96 73 29
  − 45 − 8 − 33 − 52 − 21

Subtracting 2-Digit Numbers

Write the difference. Subtract the ones column first.

ones column ↓

1.   78   36   95   17   84
   − 14   − 21   − 11   − 12   − 42
     64

2.   20   75   60   95   84
   − 20   − 22   − 50   − 41   − 62

3.   16   38   78   55   45
   − 3   − 25   − 27   − 24   − 24

4.   75   80   20   68   62
   − 54   − 10   − 10   − 11   − 51

5.   47   66   54   88   57
   − 24   − 32   − 21   − 17   − 36

Writing Numbers: 400 to 449

Start with 400. Write to 449.

400					

Writing Numbers: 450 to 499

Start with 450. Write to 499.

450				

Subtracting 3-Digit Numbers

Solve each problem below. Subtract the ones column first, then the tens column. Subtract the hundreds column last.

hundreds ↓ ↓ tens

1. 864   286   648   984   748
   −123   −133   −141   −400   −124
   ────
    741

2. 576   698   379   840   695
   −201   −568   −141   −130   −645

3. 127   762   844   539   775
   − 13   −241   −523   −425   −225

4. 572   937   623   254   742
   −122   −725   −102   − 12   −112

5. 670   938   263   400   624
   −240   −526   −142   −200   −512

30

Subtraction Booster—Grade 2   1-59441-342-8

Subtracting 3-Digit Numbers

Solve each problem below.

1.   245   667   263   314   867
    − 124   − 324   − 152   − 13   − 120
     121

2.   678   912   777   309   299
    − 542   − 801   − 245   − 103   − 46

3.   286   352   468   258   951
    − 233   − 230   − 327   − 134   − 900

4.   486   592   579   368   279
    − 322   − 371   − 263   − 122   − 100

Dot-to-Dot

Brain Teasers

Connect the dots. Count by 5s backwards.
Start at 100 and end at zero!

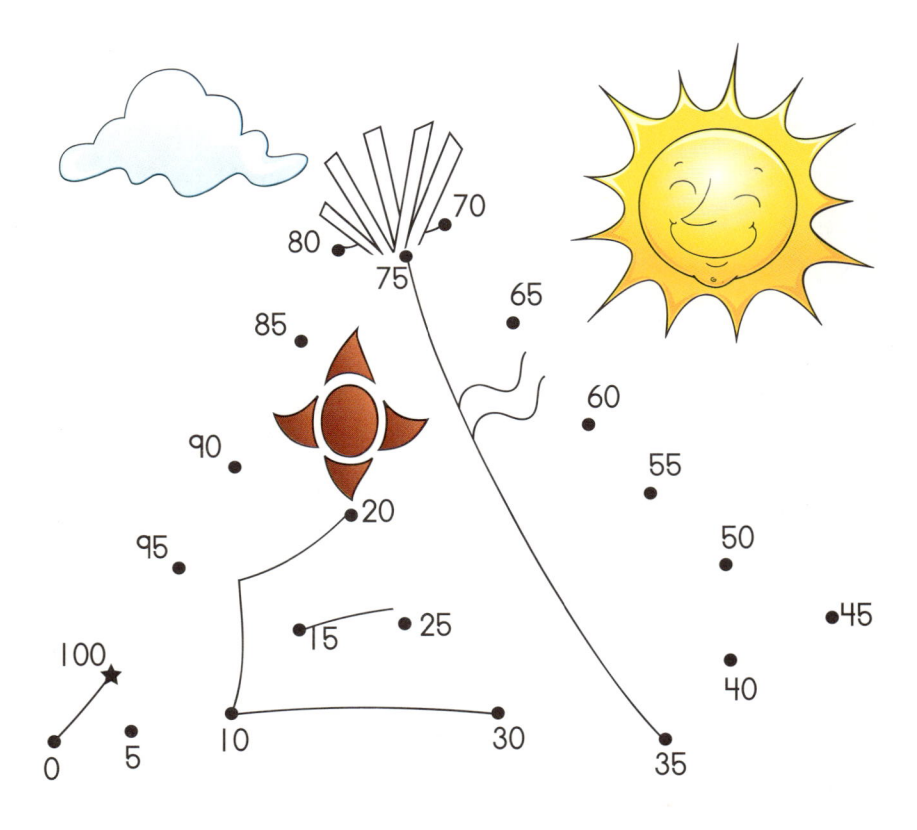

Factoid!

In 1960, Theresa and Mary Thompson, ages 8 and 9, invented and patented a solar tepee for a science fair project. They called it the "wigwarm."

Subtraction Booster—Grade 2

1-59441-342-8

Money Math

Brain Teasers

Lisa, Dianne, and Mike went to the pet store. They each had $5.00 to spend. Lisa bought 2 goldfish. Dianne bought a puppy. Mike bought a kitten. Use the cost of each animal to decide who had the most money left over.

Puppies $2.50 each

Kittens $ 3.00 each

Fish $1.00 each

Circle the animals that did not get bought.

Factoid!

There are three states in America that do NOT change their clocks during Daylight Savings Time. Can you guess which ones they are?

Answer: Indiana, Arizona, and Hawaii are always on Standard Daylight Time.

Telling Time

BRAIN TEASERS

Write the time shown on these clocks. Fill in each blank.

1.

__8:15__, or __15__ minutes after __8__ o'clock.

2.

_____, or ____ minutes after _____ o'clock.

3.

_____, or ____ minutes after _____ o'clock.

4.

_____, or ____ minutes after _____ o'clock.

Picture Problems

Brain Teasers

How many peanuts did the elephant eat?
Solve the equations below to find your answer.
Circle the peanut with the correct answer.

$92-16=\_\_$ $\_\_-27=\_\_$ $\_\_-15=\_\_$ $\_\_-4=15$

15

13

17

32

12

27

20

Greater Than or Less Than

Brain Teasers

Put the greater than (>) or less than (<) sign
in the boxes to complete the problems.

1. 14 < 19   16 ☐ 17   12 ☐ 8   17 ☐ 18
2. 10 ☐ 9   11 ☐ 6   0 ☐ 1   15 ☐ 7

This bag has black and white marbles in it. Look closely at the marbles. If you could reach in the bag and take out a handful, do you think you would have more black or more white marbles? _____

Why? _____

_____

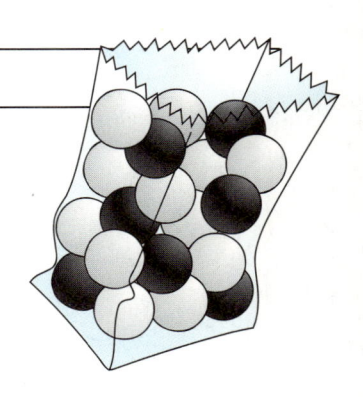

Popcorn Problems

BRAIN TEASERS

Solve each equation. Circle the kernels with a difference of an odd number.

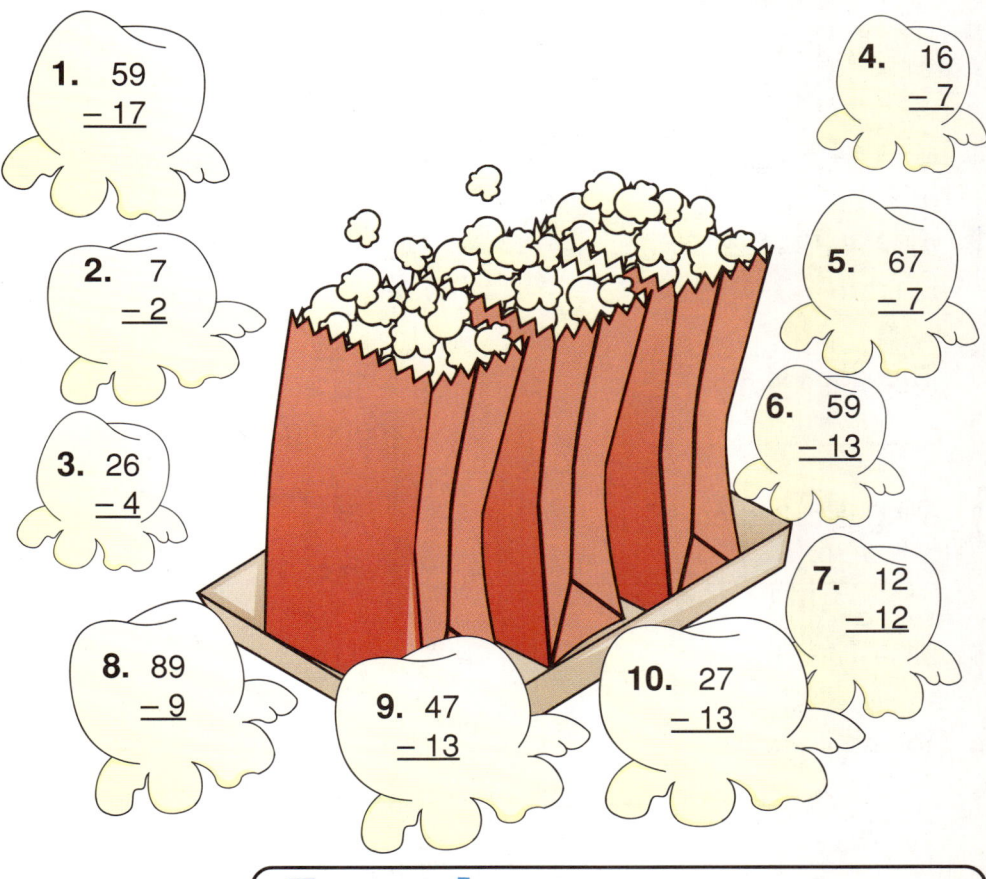

1. 59 − 17

2. 7 − 2

3. 26 − 4

4. 16 − 7

5. 67 − 7

6. 59 − 13

7. 12 − 12

8. 89 − 9

9. 47 − 13

10. 27 − 13

Factoid!
American colonists used to make "cereal" by pouring cream over popcorn and serving it for breakfast.

Crossword Puzzle: Part 1

Brain Teasers

Complete the puzzle on the next page.

Across

1. 17 – 14 = _____

2. Kids go to _____ to learn.

3. This book is about _____.

4. 5 – 3 is called an _____.

5. 56 – 47 = _____

6. To find the answer is to _____ the equation.

Down

1. You have _____ eyes.

2. The number of months in a year minus one. _____

3. Something that tells time. _____

4. 9 is an odd _____.

5. 27 – 11 = _____

6. The _____ on a clock tell you what time it is.

		Word Bank			
three	school	subtraction	equation	nine	solve
clock	eleven	sixteen	number	two	hands

Crossword Puzzle: Part 3

BRAIN TEASERS

Complete the puzzle using the clues on the previous page.

Factoid!

Question:
You have more than 100,000 hairs on your head. How many hairs do you lose each day?

Answer: 50 to 100 hairs per day.

Subtracting 3-Digit Numbers

Read the story. Write the problem and the answer in the box or on the line.

1. We went on a trip last summer. The first day we drove 241 miles, and on the second day we drove 452 miles. How many more miles did we drive on the second day?

   $$\begin{array}{r} 452 \\ -241 \\ \hline 211 \end{array}$$

   _____ miles

2. Mrs. Hill had 567 candles for sale in her store. By the end of the day, she had sold 325. How many candles did she have left?

   _____ candles left

3. There were 160 people in the park on Monday. On Friday there were 286. How many more people were in the park on Friday than on Monday?

   _____ more people on Friday.

4. There were 724 people at the ball game. When it began to rain, 510 left. How many people were left at the game? _____ people were left.

Writing Numbers: 500 to 549

Start with 500. Write to 549.

500					

Writing Numbers: 550 to 599

Start with 550. Write to 599.

550				

Writing Numbers: 600 to 649

Start with 600. Write to 649.

600					

Writing Numbers: 650 to 699

Start with 650. Write to 699.

650					

Fractions: Identifying Fractions

Circle the fraction that tells how much is shaded.

1.

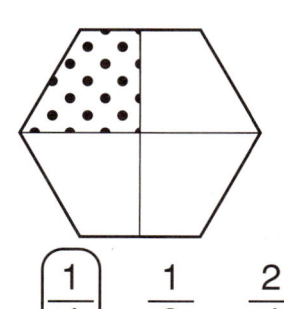

$\frac{1}{2}$ $\boxed{\frac{1}{4}}$ $\frac{1}{3}$ $\frac{2}{4}$

2.

$\frac{2}{4}$ $\frac{3}{4}$ $\frac{1}{8}$ $\frac{1}{4}$

3.

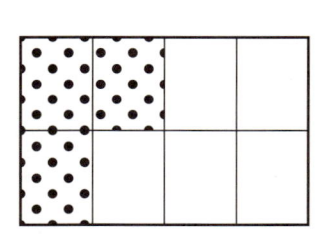

$\frac{3}{8}$ $\frac{5}{8}$ $\frac{1}{4}$ $\frac{5}{9}$

4.

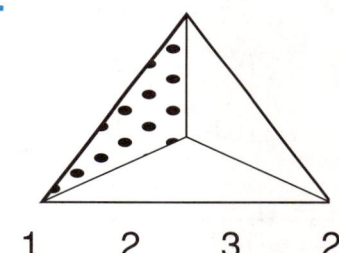

$\frac{1}{3}$ $\frac{2}{3}$ $\frac{3}{3}$ $\frac{2}{12}$

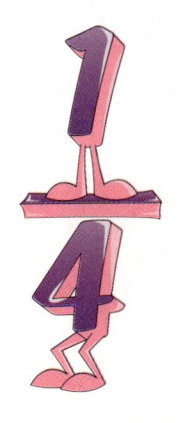

Fractions: Writing Fractions

Write the fraction in the box that tells how much is **not** shaded.

1.

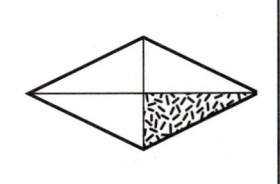

$$\frac{3}{4}$$

2.

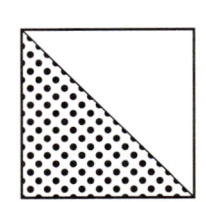

3.

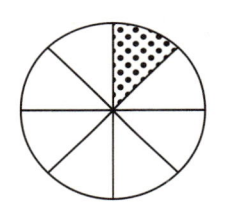

4.

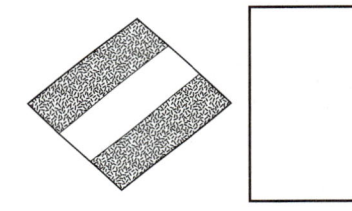

5.

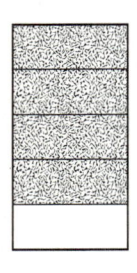

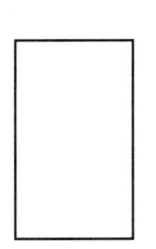

6.

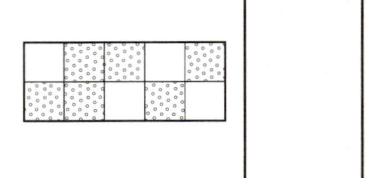

2-Digit Subtraction with Regrouping

Subtract the problems, starting in the ones place. Regroup if you need to.

1. $\overset{21}{\cancel{3}6}$ 33   51   53   84
    − 17 − 14 − 34 − 24 − 27
      19

2.   85   64   67   30   34
    − 26 − 18 − 29 − 18 − 17

3.   61   43   20   35   43
    − 32 − 34 − 12 − 16 − 28

4.   83   52   63   77   66
    − 55 − 35 − 26 − 38 − 48

5.   65   31   52   78   83
    − 17 − 24 − 14 − 29 − 26

47

1-59441-342-8   Subtraction Booster—Grade 2

2-Digit Subtraction with Regrouping

Subtract the problems, starting in the ones place. Regroup if you need to.

1. $\begin{array}{r} \overset{81}{\cancel{9}6} \\ -\ 28 \\ \hline 68 \end{array}$ $\begin{array}{r} 84 \\ -\ 39 \\ \hline \end{array}$ $\begin{array}{r} 47 \\ -\ 18 \\ \hline \end{array}$ $\begin{array}{r} 64 \\ -\ 47 \\ \hline \end{array}$ $\begin{array}{r} 22 \\ -\ 8 \\ \hline \end{array}$

2. $\begin{array}{r} 95 \\ -\ 47 \\ \hline \end{array}$ $\begin{array}{r} 14 \\ -\ 9 \\ \hline \end{array}$ $\begin{array}{r} 24 \\ -\ 10 \\ \hline \end{array}$ $\begin{array}{r} 26 \\ -\ 15 \\ \hline \end{array}$ $\begin{array}{r} 31 \\ -\ 17 \\ \hline \end{array}$

3. $\begin{array}{r} 62 \\ -\ 36 \\ \hline \end{array}$ $\begin{array}{r} 85 \\ -\ 46 \\ \hline \end{array}$ $\begin{array}{r} 74 \\ -\ 28 \\ \hline \end{array}$ $\begin{array}{r} 72 \\ -\ 8 \\ \hline \end{array}$ $\begin{array}{r} 80 \\ -\ 18 \\ \hline \end{array}$

4. $\begin{array}{r} 75 \\ -\ 38 \\ \hline \end{array}$ $\begin{array}{r} 16 \\ -\ 9 \\ \hline \end{array}$ $\begin{array}{r} 65 \\ -\ 16 \\ \hline \end{array}$ $\begin{array}{r} 18 \\ -\ 9 \\ \hline \end{array}$ $\begin{array}{r} 42 \\ -\ 28 \\ \hline \end{array}$

5. $\begin{array}{r} 51 \\ -\ 42 \\ \hline \end{array}$ $\begin{array}{r} 45 \\ -\ 26 \\ \hline \end{array}$ $\begin{array}{r} 71 \\ -\ 12 \\ \hline \end{array}$ $\begin{array}{r} 82 \\ -\ 16 \\ \hline \end{array}$ $\begin{array}{r} 48 \\ -\ 16 \\ \hline \end{array}$

2-Digit Subtraction with Regrouping

Subtract the problems, starting in the ones place. Regroup if you need to.

1. $\begin{array}{r} \overset{5\ 1}{\cancel{6}\cancel{1}} \\ -\ 33 \\ \hline \mathbf{28} \end{array}$ $\begin{array}{r} 50 \\ -13 \\ \hline \end{array}$ $\begin{array}{r} 62 \\ -\ 3 \\ \hline \end{array}$ $\begin{array}{r} 72 \\ -14 \\ \hline \end{array}$ $\begin{array}{r} 31 \\ -18 \\ \hline \end{array}$

2. $\begin{array}{r} 47 \\ -29 \\ \hline \end{array}$ $\begin{array}{r} 43 \\ -31 \\ \hline \end{array}$ $\begin{array}{r} 71 \\ -35 \\ \hline \end{array}$ $\begin{array}{r} 90 \\ -55 \\ \hline \end{array}$ $\begin{array}{r} 61 \\ -19 \\ \hline \end{array}$

3. $\begin{array}{r} 58 \\ -29 \\ \hline \end{array}$ $\begin{array}{r} 32 \\ -13 \\ \hline \end{array}$ $\begin{array}{r} 82 \\ -36 \\ \hline \end{array}$ $\begin{array}{r} 81 \\ -28 \\ \hline \end{array}$ $\begin{array}{r} 33 \\ -15 \\ \hline \end{array}$

4. $\begin{array}{r} 50 \\ -35 \\ \hline \end{array}$ $\begin{array}{r} 77 \\ -39 \\ \hline \end{array}$ $\begin{array}{r} 91 \\ -34 \\ \hline \end{array}$ $\begin{array}{r} 20 \\ -\ 2 \\ \hline \end{array}$ $\begin{array}{r} 72 \\ -\ 4 \\ \hline \end{array}$

5. $\begin{array}{r} 26 \\ -18 \\ \hline \end{array}$ $\begin{array}{r} 53 \\ -36 \\ \hline \end{array}$ $\begin{array}{r} 42 \\ -37 \\ \hline \end{array}$ $\begin{array}{r} 44 \\ -25 \\ \hline \end{array}$ $\begin{array}{r} 27 \\ -\ 4 \\ \hline \end{array}$

2-Digit Subtraction with Some Regrouping

Subtract. Regroup if you need to.

1. $\begin{array}{r} \overset{2}{\cancel{3}}\overset{1}{4} \\ -\ 18 \\ \hline 16 \end{array}$ $\begin{array}{r} 51 \\ -\ 38 \\ \hline \end{array}$ $\begin{array}{r} 42 \\ -\ 16 \\ \hline \end{array}$ $\begin{array}{r} 38 \\ -\ 22 \\ \hline \end{array}$ $\begin{array}{r} 49 \\ -\ 28 \\ \hline \end{array}$

2. $\begin{array}{r} 25 \\ -\ 13 \\ \hline \end{array}$ $\begin{array}{r} 30 \\ -\ 19 \\ \hline \end{array}$ $\begin{array}{r} 56 \\ -\ 42 \\ \hline \end{array}$ $\begin{array}{r} 83 \\ -\ 38 \\ \hline \end{array}$ $\begin{array}{r} 77 \\ -\ 44 \\ \hline \end{array}$

3. $\begin{array}{r} 16 \\ -\ 8 \\ \hline \end{array}$ $\begin{array}{r} 33 \\ -\ 30 \\ \hline \end{array}$ $\begin{array}{r} 88 \\ -\ 38 \\ \hline \end{array}$ $\begin{array}{r} 64 \\ -\ 25 \\ \hline \end{array}$ $\begin{array}{r} 23 \\ -\ 20 \\ \hline \end{array}$

4. $\begin{array}{r} 44 \\ -\ 26 \\ \hline \end{array}$ $\begin{array}{r} 75 \\ -\ 67 \\ \hline \end{array}$ $\begin{array}{r} 23 \\ -\ 13 \\ \hline \end{array}$ $\begin{array}{r} 67 \\ -\ 39 \\ \hline \end{array}$ $\begin{array}{r} 84 \\ -\ 15 \\ \hline \end{array}$

5. $\begin{array}{r} 63 \\ -\ 47 \\ \hline \end{array}$ $\begin{array}{r} 24 \\ -\ 14 \\ \hline \end{array}$ $\begin{array}{r} 27 \\ -\ 9 \\ \hline \end{array}$ $\begin{array}{r} 76 \\ -\ 17 \\ \hline \end{array}$ $\begin{array}{r} 54 \\ -\ 18 \\ \hline \end{array}$

2-Digit Subtraction with Some Regrouping

Subtract. Regroup if you need to.

1.   48   32   16   57   61
    − 28   − 13   − 9   − 45   − 28
      20

2.   95   67   47   51   93
    − 27   − 27   − 19   − 33   − 46

3.   24   60   36   57   25
    − 15   − 37   − 13   − 28   − 15

4.   60   88   65   46   21
    − 42   − 46   − 48   − 32   − 15

5.   55   67   82   48   22
    − 15   − 27   − 16   − 17   − 17

Problem Solving

Subtract and write the answers on the lines. Circle the problems in each box that have the same answer.

1.

24 − 12 = **12**

39 − 27 = _____

16 − 12 = _____

47 − 44 = _____

50 − 38 = _____

22 − 11 = _____

2.

67 − 29 = _____

21 − 9 = _____

43 − 26 = _____

55 − 38 = _____

72 − 14 = _____

33 − 16 = _____

3.

42 − 16 = _____

94 − 68 = _____

32 − 14 = _____

17 − 16 = _____

87 − 61 = _____

36 − 10 = _____

4.

44 − 19 = _____

32 − 11 = _____

61 − 31 = _____

24 − 22 = _____

55 − 25 = _____

48 − 18 = _____

Subtraction Booster—Grade 2

Word Problem Solving

Read the story. Write the problem and answer in the box.

1. We put 42 cans of fruit on the shelf. A lady bought 14 of them. How many cans are left on the shelf?

42
− 14
28

2. Dianne's box of animal crackers had 41 crackers. Mike's box had 67. How many more did he have?

3. I lined up 52 dominoes. 14 of them did not fall over. How many dominoes did fall?

4. Lisa is going on a trip for 21 days this year. Last year she went for 18 days. How many more days will she be on her trip this year than last year?

Word Problem Solving

Read the story. Write the problem and answer in the box.

1. We counted 84 peaches on our tree. Some fell off. There are still 68 on the tree. How many fell off?

   84
   − 68
   16

2. My friend and I tried to guess how many jelly beans were in a bag at the store. I guessed 48, my friend guessed 97. How many more did she guess?

3. Anna collected 78 bottle caps. Rex collected 29 fewer than Anna. How many did Rex collect?

4. After school on Tuesday, 86 children went swimming. 19 of them left before the others. How many were still left in the pool?

Problem Solving

Subtract and write the answers on the lines. Circle the problems in each box that have the same answer.

1.
54 − 19 = _____
51 − 38 = _____
62 − 30 = _____
43 − 26 = _____
26 − 13 = _____
44 − 40 = _____

2.
75 − 33 = _____
71 − 23 = _____
90 − 50 = _____
77 − 57 = _____
38 − 24 = _____
87 − 45 = _____

3.
15 − 12 = _____
59 − 56 = _____
21 − 18 = _____
38 − 35 = _____
45 − 42 = _____
18 − 9 = _____

4.
94 − 18 = _____
49 − 24 = _____
38 − 13 = _____
82 − 47 = _____
52 − 27 = _____
67 − 42 = _____

3-Digit Subtraction with Regrouping

Subtract the problems, starting in the ones place. Regroup if you need to.

1.
$$\begin{array}{r} {}^{5\ 11\ 1}\!\!\not{6}\not{2}\not{4} \\ -\ 135 \\ \hline \mathbf{489} \end{array}$$

$$\begin{array}{r} 162 \\ -\ 13 \\ \hline \end{array}$$

$$\begin{array}{r} 609 \\ -\ 319 \\ \hline \end{array}$$

$$\begin{array}{r} 378 \\ -\ 179 \\ \hline \end{array}$$

$$\begin{array}{r} 809 \\ -\ 512 \\ \hline \end{array}$$

2.
$$\begin{array}{r} 564 \\ -\ 377 \\ \hline \end{array}$$

$$\begin{array}{r} 850 \\ -\ 8 \\ \hline \end{array}$$

$$\begin{array}{r} 269 \\ -\ 94 \\ \hline \end{array}$$

$$\begin{array}{r} 460 \\ -\ 278 \\ \hline \end{array}$$

$$\begin{array}{r} 648 \\ -\ 129 \\ \hline \end{array}$$

3.
$$\begin{array}{r} 528 \\ -\ 134 \\ \hline \end{array}$$

$$\begin{array}{r} 437 \\ -\ 129 \\ \hline \end{array}$$

$$\begin{array}{r} 644 \\ -\ 246 \\ \hline \end{array}$$

$$\begin{array}{r} 434 \\ -\ 225 \\ \hline \end{array}$$

$$\begin{array}{r} 942 \\ -\ 367 \\ \hline \end{array}$$

4.
$$\begin{array}{r} 410 \\ -\ 132 \\ \hline \end{array}$$

$$\begin{array}{r} 840 \\ -\ 38 \\ \hline \end{array}$$

$$\begin{array}{r} 864 \\ -\ 239 \\ \hline \end{array}$$

$$\begin{array}{r} 717 \\ -\ 226 \\ \hline \end{array}$$

$$\begin{array}{r} 547 \\ -\ 139 \\ \hline \end{array}$$

5.
$$\begin{array}{r} 236 \\ -\ 129 \\ \hline \end{array}$$

$$\begin{array}{r} 133 \\ -\ 24 \\ \hline \end{array}$$

$$\begin{array}{r} 519 \\ -\ 287 \\ \hline \end{array}$$

$$\begin{array}{r} 933 \\ -\ 100 \\ \hline \end{array}$$

$$\begin{array}{r} 296 \\ -\ 137 \\ \hline \end{array}$$

Subtraction Booster—Grade 2

1-59441-342-8

3-Digit Subtraction with Regrouping

Subtract the problems, starting in the ones place. Regroup if you need to.

1.
$$\begin{array}{r}{\overset{6\,1}{8\!\!\!/\!5}}\\-\,406\\\hline\mathbf{469}\end{array}$$

  $$\begin{array}{r}141\\-57\\\hline\end{array}$$

  $$\begin{array}{r}843\\-327\\\hline\end{array}$$

  $$\begin{array}{r}648\\-252\\\hline\end{array}$$

  $$\begin{array}{r}286\\-137\\\hline\end{array}$$

2.
  $$\begin{array}{r}984\\-296\\\hline\end{array}$$

  $$\begin{array}{r}885\\-147\\\hline\end{array}$$

  $$\begin{array}{r}671\\-366\\\hline\end{array}$$

  $$\begin{array}{r}352\\-204\\\hline\end{array}$$

  $$\begin{array}{r}622\\-144\\\hline\end{array}$$

3.
  $$\begin{array}{r}142\\-36\\\hline\end{array}$$

  $$\begin{array}{r}328\\-182\\\hline\end{array}$$

  $$\begin{array}{r}555\\-388\\\hline\end{array}$$

  $$\begin{array}{r}210\\-97\\\hline\end{array}$$

  $$\begin{array}{r}332\\-146\\\hline\end{array}$$

4.
  $$\begin{array}{r}300\\-132\\\hline\end{array}$$

  $$\begin{array}{r}379\\-289\\\hline\end{array}$$

  $$\begin{array}{r}521\\-139\\\hline\end{array}$$

  $$\begin{array}{r}110\\-79\\\hline\end{array}$$

  $$\begin{array}{r}213\\-142\\\hline\end{array}$$

5.
  $$\begin{array}{r}216\\-139\\\hline\end{array}$$

  $$\begin{array}{r}777\\-532\\\hline\end{array}$$

  $$\begin{array}{r}824\\-57\\\hline\end{array}$$

  $$\begin{array}{r}319\\-216\\\hline\end{array}$$

  $$\begin{array}{r}469\\-122\\\hline\end{array}$$

3-Digit Subtraction with Some Regrouping

Subtract the problems, starting in the ones place. Regroup if you need to.

1.
$$\begin{array}{r} {}^{5}1\!\!\!\!/6{}^{1}\!\!\!\!/8 \\ -\ 29 \\ \hline 139 \end{array}$$

   422 − 145

   122 − 12

   325 − 132

   745 − 146

2.
   109 − 98

   229 − 149

   670 − 384

   639 − 327

   129 − 30

3.
   243 − 138

   111 − 62

   775 − 187

   622 − 219

   330 − 129

4.
   148 − 48

   394 − 139

   227 − 72

   136 − 134

   296 − 98

5.
   480 − 246

   147 − 64

   336 − 136

   126 − 113

   648 − 154

Answer Pages

Page 3
1. 9, 0, 6, 3, 6
2. 1, 11, 1, 3, 6
3. 10, 2, 5, 3, 6
4. 4, 9, 1, 1, 5
5. 12, 4, 0, 0 , 3

Page 4
1. 8, 5, 3, 0, 8
2. 0, 1, 7, 2, 0
3. 6, 4, 8, 2, 1
4. 6, 4, 5, 3, 3
5. 2, 7, 4, 9, 2

Page 5
1. 10, 4, 8, 8, 2, 3
2. 6, 3, 3, 0, 1, 5
3. 2, 1, 0, 4, 7, 7
4. 6, 3, 0, 10, 0, 2

Page 6
1. 10, 2, 5, 7, 0, 9
2. 3, 7, 1, 11, 5, 7
3. 0, 1, 9, 4, 4, 7
4. 2, 7, 4, 0, 7, 1

Page 7

0	1	2	3	4	5	6	7	8	9
10	11	12	13	14	15	16	17	18	19
20	21	22	23	24	25	26	27	28	29
30	31	32	33	34	35	36	37	38	39
40	41	42	43	44	45	46	47	48	49

1. 46
2. 10
3. 28
4. 33

Page 8

50	51	52	53	54	55	56	57	58	59
60	61	62	63	64	65	66	67	68	69
70	71	72	73	74	75	76	77	78	79
80	81	82	83	84	85	86	87	88	89
90	91	92	93	94	95	96	97	98	99

1. 52, 54, 56, 58
2. 83, 85, 87, 89
3. 66

Page 9
1. 3, 7, 2, 0, 1
2. 3, 7, 7, 4, 3
3. 2, 0, 3, 6, 8
4. 4, 0, 4, 6, 11
5. 3, 4, 4, 4, 8

Page 10
1. 9 − 7 = 2
2. 5 − 3 = 2
3. 10 − 7 = 3
4. 12 − 6 = 6

Page 11

100	101	102	103	104	105	106	107	108	109
110	111	112	113	114	115	116	117	118	119
120	121	122	123	124	125	126	127	128	129
130	131	132	133	134	135	136	137	138	139
140	141	142	143	144	145	146	147	148	149

Page 12

150	151	152	153	154	155	156	157	158	159
160	161	162	163	164	165	166	167	168	169
170	171	172	173	174	175	176	177	178	179
180	181	182	183	184	185	186	187	188	189
190	191	192	193	194	195	196	197	198	199

Answer Pages

Page 13
1. 7, 6, 12, 0, 11
2. 3, 14, 0, 4, 13
3. 17, 6, 11, 7, 16
4. 7, 9, 4, 2, 16

Page 14
1. 9, 11, 2, 9, 3
2. 17, 5, 13, 9, 4
3. 2, 7, 11, 6, 6
4. 3, 4, 11, 2, 14
5. 6, 0, 8, 15, 8

Page 15

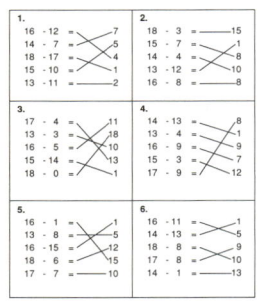

1.	2.
16 - 12 = 7 14 - 7 = 5 18 - 17 = 4 15 - 10 = 1 13 - 11 = 2	18 - 3 = 15 15 - 7 = 8 14 - 4 = 10 13 - 12 = 8 16 - 8 =
3.	4.
17 - 4 = 11 13 - 3 = 18 16 - 5 = 10 15 - 14 = 13 18 - 0 = 1	14 - 13 = 8 13 - 4 = 1 16 - 9 = 9 15 - 3 = 7 17 - 9 = 12
5.	6.
16 - 1 = 1 13 - 8 = 5 16 - 15 = 12 18 - 6 = 15 17 - 7 = 10	16 - 11 = 1 14 - 13 = 5 18 - 8 = 9 17 - 8 = 10 14 - 1 = 13

Page 16

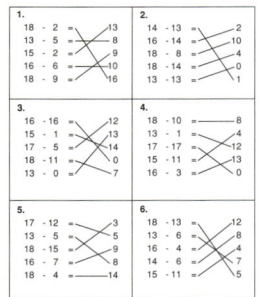

1.	2.
18 - 2 = 13 13 - 5 = 8 15 - 2 = 9 16 - 6 = 10 18 - 9 = 16	14 - 13 = 2 16 - 14 = 10 18 - 8 = 4 18 - 14 = 9 13 - 13 = 1
3.	4.
16 - 16 = 12 15 - 1 = 13 17 - 5 = 14 18 - 11 = 0 13 - 0 = 7	18 - 10 = 8 13 - 1 = 4 17 - 17 = 12 15 - 11 = 13 16 - 3 = 0
5.	6.
17 - 12 = 3 13 - 5 = 5 18 - 15 = 9 16 - 7 = 8 18 - 4 = 14	18 - 13 = 12 13 - 6 = 8 16 - 4 = 4 14 - 6 = 7 15 - 11 = 5

Page 17
1. 6, 18, 7, 1, 5
2. 14, 8, 0, 7, 9
3. 10, 3, 2, 6, 3
4. 7, 0, 15, 9, 16
5. 12, 5, 10, 10, 9
6. 5, 8, 6, 8, 9

Page 18
1. 13, 11, 3, 6, 3
2. 8, 1, 7, 5, 11
3. 7, 3, 11, 18, 14
4. 17, 0, 8, 12, 7
5. 12, 11, 8, 9, 7

Page 19

200	201	202	203	204	205	206	207	208	209
210	211	212	213	214	215	216	217	218	219
220	221	222	223	224	225	226	227	228	229
230	231	232	233	234	235	236	237	238	239
240	241	242	243	244	245	246	247	248	249

Page 20

250	251	252	253	254	255	256	257	258	259
260	261	262	263	264	265	266	267	268	269
270	271	272	273	274	275	276	277	278	279
280	281	282	283	284	285	286	287	288	289
290	291	292	293	294	295	296	297	298	299

Page 21
1. 3 hours
2. 2 hours
3. 11 children
4. 3 pages

Subtraction Booster—Grade 2

1-59441-342-8

Answer Pages

Page 22
1. 1, 10, 6, 4, 9
2. 5, 0, 11, 7, 2, 8
3. 3, 14, 30, 16, 50
4. 31, 13, 43, 89, 24
5. 75, 29, 67, 18, 68
6. 99, 15, 88, 100, 17

Page 23

300	301	302	303	304	305	306	307	308	309
310	311	312	313	314	315	316	317	318	319
320	321	322	323	324	325	326	327	328	329
330	331	332	333	334	335	336	337	338	339
340	341	342	343	344	345	346	347	348	349

Page 24

350	351	352	353	354	355	356	357	358	359
360	361	362	363	364	365	366	367	368	369
370	371	372	373	374	375	376	377	378	379
380	381	382	383	384	385	386	387	388	389
390	391	392	393	394	395	396	397	398	399

Page 25
1. 10, 40, 51, 31, 55
2. 14, 20, 23, 13, 10
3. 6, 16, 50, 23, 44
4. 10, 44, 64, 22, 50
5. 22, 40, 83, 32, 55

Page 26
1. 3, 51, 13, 40, 22
2. 1, 10, 52, 51, 16
3. 12, 20, 2, 5, 31
4. 40, 1, 15, 72, 45
5. 30, 11, 63, 21, 8

Page 27
1. 64, 15, 84, 5, 42
2. 0, 53, 10, 54, 22
3. 13, 13, 51, 31, 21
4. 21, 70, 10, 57, 11
5. 23, 34, 33, 71, 21

Page 28

400	401	402	403	404	405	406	407	408	409
410	411	412	413	414	415	416	417	418	419
420	421	422	423	424	425	426	427	428	429
430	431	432	433	434	435	436	437	438	439
440	441	442	443	444	445	446	447	448	449

Page 29

450	451	452	453	454	455	456	457	458	459
460	461	462	463	464	465	466	467	468	469
470	471	472	473	474	475	476	477	478	479
480	481	482	483	484	485	486	487	488	489
490	491	492	493	494	495	496	497	498	499

Page 30
1. 741, 153, 507, 584, 624
2. 375, 130, 238, 710, 50
3. 114, 521, 321, 114, 550
4. 450, 212, 521, 242, 630
5. 430, 412, 121, 200, 112

Page 31
1. 121, 343, 111, 301, 747
2. 136, 111, 532, 206, 253
3. 53, 122, 141, 124, 51
4. 164, 221, 316, 246, 179

Page 32
The picture is a tepee!

Answer Pages

Page 33
Lisa had the most left over. Her two goldfish cost $2.00 together. ($5–$2=$3)

Page 34
1. 8:15, or 15 minutes after 8 o'clock
2. 1:40, or 40 minutes after 1 o'clock
3. 11:20, or 20 minutes after 11 o'clock
4. 1:15, or 15 minutes after 1 o'clock

Page 35
The answer is 15.

Page 36
1. 14<19   16<17   12>8   17<18
2. 10>9   11>6   0<1   15>7

Marbles: White — because there are more white marbles in the bag.

Page 37
1. 42   2. 5   3. 22   4. 9
5. 60   6. 46   7. 0   8. 80
9. 34   10. 14

Page 38
Across:
1. three   2. school   3. subtraction
4. equation 5. nine   6. solve

Down:
1. two   2. eleven   3. clock
4. number   5. sixteen 6. hands

Page 39

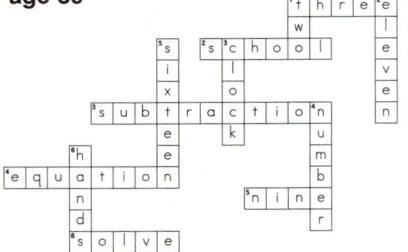

(crossword puzzle solution with answers: three, school, subtraction, equation, nine, solve, two, eleven, clock, number, sixteen, hands)

Page 40
1. 452–241=211   2. 567–325=242
3. 286–160=126   4. 724–510=214

Page 41

500	501	502	503	504	505	506	507	508	509
510	511	512	513	514	515	516	517	518	519
520	521	522	523	524	525	526	527	528	529
530	531	532	533	534	535	536	537	538	539
540	541	542	543	544	545	546	547	548	549

Page 42

550	551	552	553	554	555	556	557	558	559
560	561	562	563	564	565	566	567	568	569
570	571	572	573	574	575	576	577	578	579
580	581	582	583	584	585	586	587	588	589
590	591	592	593	594	595	596	597	598	599

Page 43

600	601	602	603	604	605	606	607	608	609
610	611	612	613	614	615	616	617	618	619
620	621	622	623	624	625	626	627	628	629
630	631	632	633	634	635	636	637	638	639
640	641	642	643	644	645	646	647	648	649

Page 44

650	651	652	653	654	655	656	657	658	659
660	661	662	663	664	665	666	667	668	669
670	671	672	673	674	675	676	677	678	679
680	681	682	683	684	685	686	687	688	689
690	691	692	693	694	695	696	697	698	699

Page 45
1. $\frac{1}{4}$ 2. $\frac{2}{4}$ 3. $\frac{3}{8}$ 4. $\frac{1}{3}$

Answer Pages

Page 46
1. $\frac{3}{4}$ 2. $\frac{1}{2}$ 3. $\frac{7}{8}$
4. $\frac{1}{3}$ 5. $\frac{1}{5}$ 6. $\frac{4}{10}$

Page 47
1. 19, 19, 17, 29, 57
2. 59, 46, 38, 12, 17
3. 29, 9, 8, 19, 15
4. 28, 17, 37, 39, 18
5. 48, 7, 38, 49, 57

Page 48
1. 68, 45, 29, 17, 14
2. 48, 5, 14, 11, 14
3. 26, 39, 46, 64, 62
4. 37, 7, 49, 9, 14
5. 9, 19, 59, 66, 32

Page 49
1. 28, 37, 59, 58, 13
2. 18, 12, 36, 35, 42
3. 29, 19, 46, 53, 18
4. 15, 38, 57, 18, 68
5. 8, 17, 5, 19, 23

Page 50
1. 16, 13, 26, 16, 21
2. 12, 11, 14, 45, 33
3. 8, 3, 50, 39, 3
4. 18, 8, 10, 28, 69
5. 16, 10, 18, 59, 36

Page 51
1. 20, 19, 7, 12, 33
2. 68, 40, 28, 18, 47
3. 9, 23, 23, 29, 10
4. 18, 42, 17, 14, 6
5. 40, 40, 66, 31, 5

Page 52
1. ⑫, ⑫, 4, 3, ⑫, 11
2. 38, 12, ⑰, ⑰, 58, ⑰
3. ㉖, ㉖, 18, 1, ㉖, ㉖
4. 25, 21, ㉚, 2, ㉚, ㉚

Page 53
1. 42 − 14 = 28
2. 67 − 41 = 26
3. 52 − 14 = 38
4. 21 − 18 = 3

Page 54
1. 84 − 68 = 16
2. 97 − 48 = 49
3. 78 − 29 = 49
4. 86 − 19 = 67

Page 55
1. 35, ⑬, 32, 17, ⑬, 4
2. ㊷, 48, 40, 20, 14, ㊷
3. ③, ③, ③, ③, ③, 9
4. 76, ㉕, ㉕, 35, ㉕, ㉕

Page 56
1. 489, 149, 290, 199, 297
2. 187, 842, 175, 182, 519
3. 394, 308, 398, 209, 575
4. 278, 802, 625, 491, 408
5. 107, 109, 232, 833, 159

Page 57
1. 469, 84, 516, 396, 149
2. 688, 738, 305, 148, 478
3. 106, 146, 167, 113, 186
4. 168, 90, 382, 31, 71
5. 77, 245, 767, 103, 347

Page 58
1. 139, 277, 110, 193, 599
2. 11, 80, 286, 312, 99
3. 105, 49, 588, 403, 201
4. 100, 255, 155, 2, 198
5. 234, 83, 200, 13, 494

Notes

Five things I'm thankful for:
1. _____
2. _____
3. _____
4. _____
5. _____